Nature's Gifts

Enjoy Nature!

Lee Huston

Nature's Gifts

A FAMILY FUN BOOK
Exploring Pictures, Prose, & Poetry

Harriette "Ree" Huston

TATE PUBLISHING
AND **ENTERPRISES**, LLC

Published by Tate Publishing & Enterprises, LLC
127 E. Trade Center Terrace | Mustang, Oklahoma 73064 USA
1.888.361.9473 | www.tatepublishing.com

Tate Publishing is committed to excellence in the publishing industry. The company reflects the philosophy established by the founders, based on Psalm 68:11,

"The Lord gave the word and great was the company of those who published it."

Book design copyright © 2012 by Tate Publishing, LLC. All rights reserved.
Cover design by April Marciszewski
Interior design by Lynly D. Grider

Published in the United States of America

ISBN: 978-1-61346-679-7
1. Nature, Animals, Wildlife
2. Language Arts & Disciplines, Vocabulary
12.04.13

Nature's Gifts

ACKNOWLEDGMENTS

Pictures used are courtesy of Digi Photos by Dan Huston, husband, Randy Huston, son, or when undesignated, were taken by the author. Thanks to Sally Harris for Ree and Skookum's back cover photograph.

The California quail egg was identified by volunteers at the Dungeness River Audubon Center, Sequim, Washington, 2008. Fish information was verified by Doug Morriel, Manager, Lower Elwha Klallam Tribe, Fisheries Department, Port Angeles, Washington, 2008.

Thanks to friends for reviews and constructive comments: Josephine B. Adams; Mary Beth Blake; Florence E. Evanoff, M.A., M.Div., Ed.D.; Sally Harris, Northwest children's author; Nora Rogers, BA in Math Education, M.A. in Curriculum and Instruction; and Matthew S. Niemeyer, M.D., Cataract Surgery and Glaucoma; Agnieszka J. Niemeyer, M.D., Medical, Surgical & Cosmetic Dermatology, and their young children.

Thanks for computer assistance by Mark Grime and Randy Huston.

CONTENTS

INTRODUCTION

Nature's Gifts explores both wild and domestic country animals, plants, people, and experiences. The mediums of pictures, prose, and poetry present a broad synchronized examination of tiny tastes of life.

People are increasingly building homes in what had been only territory of wild animals. Awareness and understanding of some animals nearby many homes may be increased through reading and discussion of the subjects in this book. Each chapter shows one or more gifts to us from nature. The gifts may include animals, plants, people, relationships, food, etc. Understandings may help us to all live in harmony.

Pictures and prose relate to information within each poem. Children, parents, and adults may enjoy discussing this book together at home or when traveling. Adults can read to children, listen to them read, or simply enjoy these situations for themselves. Youth "babysitting" can share this book and develop rapport with their young charges. Sharing your copy with shut-ins at home, in hospitals, or in nursing facilities will quickly start a sharing of memories. You'll both enjoy the visit more.

Poetry is simply a method of communicating thoughts and feelings from one person (the writer) to another (the reader or listener). If you read these poems aloud, you will get a broader feel of meanings and life's rhythms. The author believes she has more freedom and challenge through poetry as a medium of written communication of life experiences than through a strictly prose form of writing. The brevity and flexibility of poetry often seems a faster method of communication than prose.

Educators may find this book a helpful learning tool at many levels and in many settings. Older children will relate to the content in a different sense than younger ones. Vocabulary becomes increasingly difficult as the book progresses. You may, of course, lower or raise the vocabulary level to suit your listener.

This book could, also, prove helpful to anyone learning English as a second language. Group reading aloud, with discussion following, could prove highly beneficial. English structure continuity with its variations can be observed.

Subjects, as presented, can assist learning in new, exciting ways within familiar settings. Observation skills can be increased through picture discussions, reading aloud, and by utilizing stimulating thoughts in Springboard Jump, Let's Talk. New information perspectives can be formulated. Exposure to various methods of poetry expression can be developed. Map-reading skills can be broadened. Vocabulary may be expanded. A new appreciation of various animals or situations may develop. Do encourage and participate in fun-appropriate activities for children and/or adults. A Fun to Do activity climax for each subject will help solidify your satisfaction and reading enjoyment with learning.

There may be additional benefits. Children can learn and discuss pet care. Ways to improve personal health habits can be brought to the forefront. Broadening of writing skills can be encouraged and developed. Important rules of the road can be learned. Personal safety from many kinds of predators could be developed in "Wild Raccoons," "Backyard Sanctuary," and "Stitch in Time."

Subject matter is intended for a wide range of ages—children through the young-at-heart. Most of the guide questions in Springboard Jump will help improve comprehension. They are intended for a range of school-age children but are worth adult thoughts. Questions raised are mostly about content rather than style. Answers can be simplified or broadened into wider venues surrounding the subjects, such as creature habits, conservation, medical needs, or ecology issues. Poetry style and content could develop thought and discussion. Even trial rewrites in Fun to Do of a subject, without copying, can broaden understanding and writing skills to avoid plagiarism.

Questions will assist English language development and thought retention for all ages of people. Using your imagination as to what could have happened in each scenario could spark additional interest. Reading aloud, even to oneself, with differing vocal expressions can give a different perspective to each poem and intensify enjoyment.

Reading and discussion of the same chapter with another person has advantages. Someone of a different age or background can present a different perspective and understanding. Discussion can create a greater sense of friendship or bonding.

The author hopes you will enjoy this book on many levels, i.e., that

- you will enjoy reading the poems silently and aloud
- you will have fun
- your awareness of your surroundings is heightened
- you think of things you haven't thought of in years
- you gain at least one new insight
- your imagination takes a ride
- you enjoy this poetry with its background information
- you gain a new perspective through the questions presented
- you feel stimulated as you share chapters with children or peers
- you find opportunities for involvement in discussions or assisting others to read
- you help relieve the boredom of a home shut-in, or hospital or nursing home patient
- you enjoy making and sharing nature's gifts with children and friends
- you will feel your life is enriched from reading this book

Please Note: The Photo Gallery pictures refer to the related subject page in this book. Additionally, each chapter heading relates back to the photograph by number.

PHOTO GALLERY

Orchard Mason Bee
Nesting Blocks
Page 23

1

Red Squirrel Watching
by Digi Photos
Page 29

2

Cattails in a Marsh
Page 33

3

Alert Deer by Randy Huston Page 37

4

Hand-Decorated Chicken Eggs Page 41

5

How to Make a Leaf Cup Page 49

6

HARRIETTE "REE" HUSTON

*Skookum Enjoying
White Heather by
Digi Photos
Page 55*

7

*Highway 101 East of
Sequim, Washington,
and Walking Trail
Bridge by Digi Photos
Page 59*

8

*Weir to Catch Salmon
with Reflected Bridge
by Digi Photos
Page 59*

9

NATURE'S GIFTS

Steller's Jay by
Digi Photos
Page 65

10

11

Pine Siskins Eating
Thistle Seeds by
Digi Photos
Page 65

Wild Raccoon by
Digi Photos
Page 73

12

HARRIETTE "REE" HUSTON

Curious Chickens
Page 79

13

Crows in a Tree
by Digi Photos
Page 83

14

Tree Shadows
Bar Code
Page 89

15

A Fun Sachet
Page 95

16

Honeybee Feasting
on Lavender by
Digi Photos
Page 99

17

Preserved
Humming Birds
Page 105

18

HARRIETTE "REE" HUSTON

Yard Bat Houses
Page 109

19

California Quail
Egg Shell
Page 115

20

Frog by a Rhododendron Floweret Page 121

21

Cookie Treats by Digi Photos Page 135

22

HARRIETTE "REE" HUSTON

ORCHARD MASON BEES

Kick It Around

Photo 1

Mason bees are wild bees that live in wooden holes near water all over the U.S.A. They appear to be like tiny flies. The ones near Sequim, Washington, appear black. They do not make hives or attack in mass. Their four wings and six legs are like all bees. Only the female can sting (like a mosquito bite).

They come out of *hibernation* (sleep) from their holes and are active before other bees. Their early spring appearance and their tiny size are why mason bees are able to spread *pollen* to about 95 percent to 99 percent of fruit flowers so that fruit will grow. This happens while they gather pollen and sweet *nectar* for food for their own eggs when they hatch.

A nesting block can be handmade from thick, untreated, good quality, dry (not cedar) wood drilled with holes five-sixteenths of an inch in diameter as shown in photo 1. Place it in a sunny, protected place. In the wild, properly sized natural or beetle holes are used. Only one white, three-millimeter-long, weiner-shaped, female egg is deposited by a female mason bee at the back of each hole on a paste of nectar and pollen. After this hole is sealed with about one-fourth-inch of mud, each male mason bee egg is laid on its food and sealed. A female mason bee lays about thirty-five eggs during her short life—two-thirds to three-fourths of them are male. Queens take fourteen to thirty-five trips to collect food plus take eight to twelve more trips to collect mud to prepare each egg's nest. There are no designated worker bees—just queens work.

Soon after each egg is safely covered, it will slowly change into worm-like *larva* over about a month. The wiggly larva will spin its cocoon, turn into a *pupa*, and then into an adult before it sleeps through the winter in the cocoon. These changes are called *metamorphosis*.

When spring weather warms to 50° Fahrenheit, the bees chew away the soft end of their cocoon. Males hatch first over a period of about ten to fifteen days, eat, mate with one or more female mason bees outside the nest, and then die. Female mason bees are gone by June.

Orchard Mason Bees

Woodpecker pecks a mason bee hole,
Trying for his reward.
Fly away, woodpecker,
Bee-babies sleeping,
Waiting for spring to arrive.

Shiny black bees crawl out of their beds,
Kiss the early tree blooms.
So tiny, gets sweetness
And deep pollen, too,
To feed new bee-babies next spring.

The queen bee lays new bee-baby eggs
On pollen nectar food.
Mud seals holes, eggs are safe
Through winter's cold gloom,
Spring, fertilized blossoms grow fruit.

Springboard Jump

Let's Talk

Who has seen a woodpecker? What did it look like?

What would be the woodpecker's reward in this poem?

Who was "shooing" away the woodpecker here?

Did you save the bee-babies? How do you know?

When—what months—would the bee-babies awaken?

Are honeybees or bumble bees active this early in the spring?

What are they doing?

How many queen bee eggs are laid in one hole?

How many male bee eggs are laid in one hole, in one series? *(a math application)*

Mason bees have no hive. What does that mean?

What takes the place of a hive?

What kinds of bees live in hives?

What happens when orchard mason bees taste the sweet fruit nectar in blossoms?

Why do we want these special tiny bees when fruit trees are blooming?

What is pollen? Where is it found?

Who brings and mixes nectar and pollen and then lays an egg?

What does mixing pollen between flowers do to help our fruit trees?

Why do mason bees do a better job mixing pollen for flowers than other bees?

How do you make mud? Why would mason bees live where water can be found?

Why does the queen use mud to seal in the pollen and nectar paste with each egg?

Why do the bee-babies need to eat?

After the bee-babies hatch, what else do they do before they crawl out of their hole?

Fun to Do

Imagination In Drawing

1. Draw a black mason bee coming out of a flower with pollen on its legs.

or

Make and Hang a Mason Bee Nesting Block

1. Use a block of wood (not cedar) and drill 5/16th inch holes to make nesting blocks. The ones shown have roofs. This is not required. Place them on the south side of the house in full sunshine.

Notchy Squirrel

Kick It Around

Photo 2

The squirrel in photo 2 is a red squirrel. Sunflower seeds in the bird food are to their liking. They also eat grains and enjoy dried corn.

Red squirrels are slightly larger than ground squirrels or chipmunks. The author, at this writing, has a tiny ground squirrel that often runs around on the house roof and in the gutter. Chipmunks are of similar size but have white stripes. Red squirrels seen on the Olympic Peninsula have all been small with thin tails. The squirrels seen in the Seattle area appear as rich red-brown and are much larger with big fluffy tails.

Notchy was a red-brown squirrel. The author's husband spent much time outside with the squirrels. They were not around much in the wintertime. Notchy and one other squirrel did become comfortable enough with him to climb up his body to get nuts from his shirt pocket. This is *not* recommended! They could bite you and give you disease.

Uninvited squirrels used the cat door to come into the house and bury nuts in the soil of houseplants. When surprised, they sometimes had trouble finding the cat door to get out. This is one of the disadvantages of pet access doors.

Additionally, they may build a nest in a warm place such as a dryer vent. This will block the flow of air in the vent to dry clothes.

Notchy Squirrel

Notchy had a notch in his ear.
He can't see well, but he can hear.
A peanut smell brings him so near,
On table, chair. *Bang!* Runs in fear.

In the trees, Notchy sits so still.
He's looking back from on the hill.
Put out more peanuts, crush for smell.
Will he come back for those that fell?

Our sunning cat without a care,
On picnic table—peanuts there.
Notchy appears, smelling for treat,
Creeps up slowly ready to eat.

Cat sees Notchy moving closer.
A la z z z y stretch, then fluffs her fur.
Nose-to-nose, Notchy sees the cat
Each takes off like an acrobat.

HARRIETTE "REE" HUSTON

Springboard Jump

Let's Talk

Why was the squirrel named Notchy?

What do squirrels like to eat?

What is Notchy doing when he sits very still?

Are squirrels as active in winter as in other seasons?

What are they doing?

What are the seasons of the year?

Where is Seattle? Where is the Olympic Peninsula?

What big body of salt water is between Seattle and the Olympic Peninsula?

How would people get from Seattle to the Olympic Peninsula?

Why do we think Notchy can't see well?

How does Notchy know there are peanuts he wants?

How do we know that it was Notchy with the cat?

Why did the cat sit so still?

What might Notchy do to save extra nuts?

What might he do later to find those extra nuts?

If you see a squirrel, how would you know if it is Notchy?

Fun to Do

Notchy Sees Toutle

    1.   Draw Notchy and the cat nose-to-nose on the picnic table.
and

    2.   Draw Notchy and the cat like acrobats.

or

Write a Poem

    1.   Write a poem about your pet or an animal you have seen.

Red-Winged Blackbirds' Family and Friends

Kick It Around

Photo 3

Red-winged blackbirds enjoy sitting in cattails. They may come singly, as a family, or in big groups. Often, they will hide in the cattail thickets for shelter to sleep at night.

These large cattails will only grow where there is standing water called *marshland*. This must be standing fresh water, not salt water. This picture shows Sequim Bay, which is salt water. (Sequim rhymes with swim.)

In the fall, cattails can be cut and dried for lovely indoor bouquets. Care must be taken to dip or spray each head in varnish or lacquer, or even use hair spray, to delay the seeds from breaking apart. Left in nature, the fluffy seeds will break out and fly away with the wind, as can be seen in the picture. The strength of nature will cause the seeds to eventually break open in the mature brown head, even if treated, although it could take a year or two.

There are *simulated* or *artificial* cattails of varying sizes that can be bought in stores to use in bouquets. Real ones are sometimes available for sale.

Red-Winged Blackbirds'
Family And Friends

See the red-winged blackbird
On a cattail?
One—two—three
Now, see family in detail.

Away flies—one—two,
Chased by another.
Beauty in their wind song,
Calling each other.

We're like the red-wings
Teasing each other.
—Come —one, —come —two, soon
Friends bond as brothers.

Friendships may be long
Or in passing short,
But mem'ries will be
The long-lasting sort.

Springboard Jump

Let's Talk

What are the blackbirds doing at the start of the poem?

What do cattails look like?

Where do they grow?

What time of year do you see a firm, brown bloom at the top of a straight stalk with leaves all around?

Would it be easy to get to them to cut? Why not?

Who has seen a real cattail or even an *artificial* one?

What does artificial mean?

What happens to the firm, brown heads in the winter?

Do they make you think of dandelion seeds? Why?

After sitting on the cattails, what did the blackbirds do?

Do you suppose they play like you play? How does the poem show them at play?

What creates the beauty? How are you aware of this kind of beauty?

What can make a wind song? How is it like this beauty?

When do you play? What are some things you do when you play outside?

What is teasing? Is it good or bad, or can it be both?

What is an example of good teasing? Bad teasing?

Is bullying good or bad? Why?

How does playing create friendships?

How long do you keep your friends?

What can cause a friendship to start or to stop?

As you get older and friends move away, how can you maintain (keep up) your friendship?

Could a friendship be called a circle of love? Why?

Are there different kinds of love? Give examples.

Fun to Do

Lunch Time Picture

1. Draw a picture of you and your friends eating lunch together: at school, home, or on a picnic. In which setting might a red-winged blackbird be present?

or

Red-winged Blackbirds Drawing

1. Draw a picture of a family of red-winged blackbirds sitting on cattails growing in a ditch.

OUR DEER FRIENDS

Kick It Around

Photo 4

Deer are beautiful creatures. We must remember, however, that they are wild. In addition, they have been known to carry disease that can make people sick. When they come into the yard of a home, they enjoy eating tender rosebuds and other prize plantings.

The deer population in the United States has *expanded*. Many states, such as Kansas, that never before had a deer population problem, now have cause for concern.

Deer, and even moose and black bear, can be hazardous on the roads. Elk herds cross roads on Washington State's Olympic Peninsula to graze in the yards of homes. There are radio-controlled, yellow, blinking lights on U.S. Highway 101 near Sequim, Washington. These lights warn motorists that elk with radio collars are within a quarter mile. Drivers often stop on the edge of the highway and get out of their cars to take pictures when the elk are in view, thus, creating another hazard to oncoming traffic.

Our Deer Friends

Olympic Mountains Hurricane Ridge
Doe and fawn with buck in foliage.
What do they eat? What do they see?
Are they afraid? They run to flee?

They are with wild animals that roam
Close by and run far from their home.
They see trees, grassy places graze,
Rocks jut out to be seen through haze.

To take their pictures, stand where you are.
Offer no food; just stay afar,
'Cause noise will make them perk their ears.
Heads go up, *whir r r*; they run with peers.

HARRIETTE "REE" HUSTON

Springboard Jump

Let's Talk

(Look on a map of the U.S.A. Find Highway 101, which runs east and west. Find the cities of Port Angeles and Sequim, Washington, near the Pacific Ocean.)

Where are the Olympic Mountains?

What family members are the doe and the fawn?

What family member is the buck?

How can you tell a deer is a buck?

How do you spell *deer*, the name of the animal?

If you love someone and you say, "Dear," how do you spell *dear*?

Do they sound the same?

What does *expand* mean?

What is foliage?

Where do deer find foliage around here?

What would deer eat on Hurricane Ridge?

How high is it? *(Look on your map.)*

What would we see at Hurricane Ridge?

Do you graze? What do you think that means?

What other animals graze?

Have you ever seen haze? Where? What is it like?

Why stand still to take pictures of the deer?

What happens when deer perk their ears?

Peers means what?

Who are deer peers?

Who are your peers?

Why would there be more traffic accidents caused by hitting deer and other wild animals on the Northeast coast of the United States?

Fun to Do

Who Am I?

1. Draw rocks on a mountain with foliage. Include a deer's head with antlers sticking up between rocks. What family member would this be?

The Vain Ostrich

Kick It Around

Photo 5

An ostrich farm had been active near Sequim, Washington. The incidents in the poem did happen on this farm.

Ostrich stand about nine feet high and have three toes. This is the earth's largest living bird and fastest two-legged animal. The tallest living flying birds are Cambodia's endangered sarus cranes.

Meat from ostrich can be made into jerky, or sold raw ground or as steaks. Their skin is sold, dried, and used for purses, belts, billfolds, etc. Feathers are soft and delicate. They are used for decoration on hats, dresses, pins, etc. Ostrich eggshells can be made into votive candleholders or painted for display (see photo 5). Their eggs are bigger than when you put your outstretched fingers and thumbs touching using both hands.

Fences must be at least eight feet high (as high as the ceiling in a home) to keep the birds from jumping them. Visitors at the farm were kept away from these birds. Ostrich could peck or slash at you with two big claws on their feet and hurt you. The ostrich farmer has to be careful to gather eggs when the hen is not on her nest; otherwise, he would get hurt as she protects her nest. Ostrich can live thirty to seventy years.

At that time, there were no government *subsidies* (money) given to help ostrich farmers in the United States. Subsidies were given by governments in Africa to ostrich farmers there. African farmers could sell their ostrich meat, etc., for much less money than could U.S.A. farmers. This drove the price down in the United States and caused this farm to close.

The Vain Ostrich

Close together some birds will fly
Like an airplane up in the sky.
Geese have a lead for their own V.
Hear them honk, now you can see.

Ostrich are birds, but they can't fly.
Wings too small, each leg a big thigh.
Long scale-like legs, feet—two clawed toes,
They make a sound but make no crows.

Its eggs are shaped like chickens lay.
Their shell so big, sixteen repay.
Paint lovely shells and then display,
People will have a lot to say.

One pecked and scared for a lady's hat.
He really wanted to have that.
When the hat was placed on his head,
He was proud of his hat of red.

Another ostrich stole a scarf
That was to be put on a hearth.
Persistent ostrich seemed to say,
Thank you—I'm beau-ti-ful today.

Springboard Jump

Let's Talk

Have you seen an ostrich? What do they look like? Are they wild animals?

What is the difference between a wild animal and a *domesticated* one?

Where does the tallest living flying bird live? *(On a world map, find Cambodia.)*

What is its name?

What does *endangered* mean?

What is the name of the largest living bird that runs very fast but doesn't fly?

Why can they not fly? How can the wings be useful to the ostrich when it runs?

What can ostrich do if they are frightened?

How many toes does an ostrich have?

How many toes have big dangerous claws? How could they hurt you?

How many chicken eggs would it take to equal an ostrich egg?

How could this big eggshell be used?

Do you feel good when you know you look nice?

How do you think the dressed-up ostrich felt?

What does *vain* mean? Is this good? What do vain and *vein*, which sound alike, mean?

How can a subsidy be helpful?

How can it be bad for a farmer?

Do you know of crops that receive subsidies now in the U.S.A.? How can it help the farmer?

Fun to Do

Make a Beautiful Decorated Eggshell

1. Have a large, washed, raw chicken or duck egg, a clean bowl to catch the egg insides, and a very large needle. Vinegar in the wash water will help cut the natural waxy surface of the egg.

2. Holding the egg, poke holes at each end of the egg as large as possible without breaking the eggshell any more than necessary. Use the needle to break up the egg yolk and white inside the egg, if need be. Gently blow on one end, holding the other end over the clean bowl that will catch the raw egg. When all of the egg is blown out of the shell, gently wash it clean, and let it dry overnight.

or

3. Use very sharp small scissors to enlarge one hole, or, instead, pierce a hole on the side and trim out an oval so that the

inside of the egg can be removed. Clean very gently, and let it dry overnight. Then, you can decorate your eggshell.

4. Decorate as-is with paint. Let it dry. Then glue on trims, sequins, bright string, rickrack, lace, etc. Glue a string hanger on one end for use as a Christmas tree ornament. Your paint helps strengthen the shell.

or

5. A blown extra large chicken or duck egg can be cut on the end or side large enough to hold a votive candle. Glue the opposite flat side down on top of a decorated jar lid so that the eggshell will not tip. Let the glue dry. Decorate the outside of the eggshell as desired. Place a votive candle in the egg. This will make a beautiful gift.

and

6. What can you do with the remaining egg?

    a. Cook as a scrambled egg to eat. Be sure to remove any eggshell,

or

    b. Use it as a baking ingredient.

or

Decorate Sugar Cookies

1. Make or buy unbaked sugar cookies. Heat the range oven. Prepare baking pans as directed.

2. Separate one egg yolk from the white. Add a tiny drop of water into each part and mix gently.

3. To make different paint colors, mix food coloring in measuring-teaspoon-size portions of the egg yolk. (The yellow yolk may change your color.)

4. Roll cookies flat, cut out designs, and place each on your greased and floured baking sheet.

5. Paint each cookie with the colored egg yolk using a new, washed, small, thin paintbrush. Wash your paintbrush after each color and before each color change or have separate new washed brushes. Allow each color to dry.

6. Paint stirred egg white over the entire cookie while moist, and quickly spread white granulated sugar over the entire top. (The damp egg white makes the sugar stay on the cookie.) Cookies can dry for a short time after sugaring until you are ready to bake a pan full.

7. Set a timer and bake, following the directions given for the cookies.

8. Share and enjoy your cookies, which through your work and ingredients, are a gift of nature. They will keep a very long time. When cooled and sealed from air, these cookies will keep best if refrigerated or frozen until they are to be served. (Note: these sugar cookies are referred to in Children, Nature's Gift, Fun to Do, Make Cookies)

Adventures of
an Ant and Leaf

Kick It Around

Photo 6

Pretty leaves have long been used for decoration on tables, around doors, etc. Flat, colored leaves can be dipped or lightly sprayed with glycerin, dried, and then may be enjoyed for years.

Photo 6 leaf cups can be made using an extra-large maple leaf, as shown, or a sycamore leaf. Gather the leaves before September to have the strongest leaves when dried. Use a fresh (not dried), *carefully cleaned* leaf so that it can be easily molded to the outside of a cup. Look at this picture. Fold to fit. No glue is used. Flat twist ties just hold the points up and prevent curling as the leaf dries. Rubber bands hold the shape.

A small leaf cup with could be made by shaping it over a tiny cup or the bottom of a small glass or a jar with straight *vertical* sides. After air-drying a week or more, each cup could be sprayed inside and later outside with sealer. The cups would then be cleaner, less fragile, and have a longer useful life.

Candy, raisins, nuts, pretzels, small gifts, name tags, Christmas ball ornaments, or other small items can be placed in the cups for a festive unique dinner table decoration. Try them under a table lamp, on a dresser holding pretty jewelry, on a desk holding paper clips, or give one to someone in a hospital with a nice written note, etc. People will enjoy the holder as well as it being nature's gift.

Adventures of an Ant and Leaf

Maple leaf dancing on the tree,
Come and journey you and me.
Your green turns red and orange and brown.
Now you've fallen upside down.

Dried like a cup, handle protrudes,
Ant crawls in to look for food.
A surprise in store when inside,
Rain comes down; both start to glide.

Leaf-cup and ant float down a stream.
It really seems like a dream.
Swirls and twirls, up and down from wind.
Ant gets seasick, leaf gets pinned.

Ant jumps away while leaf-cup waits
Your picnic to come with plates.
Ant gets a taste, then gets his friend,
Leaf-cup's found and gets a mend.

Springboard Jump

Let's Talk

Does anyone have an ant farm to watch at home? Please show it to us.

Where could this maple leaf and ant be?

Did the ant expect to travel with the leaf? What else could have happened?

Can you guess what time of year this takes place?

How many points does a maple leaf have?

What makes the maple leaf fall down? Why?

Are there other trees that have leaves that fall?

What are the names of trees that don't lose leaves, just needles?

What is unusual about this maple leaf?

What happened when the ant got inside the leaf cup?

What was the surprise for the ant?

Why would the ant enjoy or not enjoy the ride?

What stopped the enjoyment of the ant and the leaf?

Why did the leaf cup need to be mended?

What did the ant do?

What would an ant like to eat?

Was there likely more than one ant friend?

How many people would be at a picnic?

Who would have found the leaf to mend it?

What is the difference between *straight* and *vertical*?

Fun to Do

Draw a Maple Leaf

1. Draw around your hand spread as widely as possible. While tracing, draw your fingernail tips pointed—not rounded.
2. Now, draw connections between your fingers curving closer to your first joint; erase the lines below.
3. Add a line where your wrist would be.
4. Draw in a straight line from about two inches below your wrist line to the tip of your middle finger. Make this line just a little bit wider (thicker) outside of your drawn hand for a stem.
5. Draw a line from each fingertip to the center line at your wrist to make leaf veins. Doesn't your paper hand now look a lot like a maple leaf?
6. Color the leaf with fall colors. What are fall colors?
7. Draw an ant on the leaf.

or

Make a Leaf Cup as Pictured

1. Use a fresh, clean, extra-large leaf; a cup with vertical sides, rubber bands, and lots of never used twist ties.

2. Form each leaf to fit the shape of your cup or glass. The stem can be a handle by folding it upward. Hold it in place with rubber bands.

3. Fold twist ties to hold up the leaf tips. They can be held in place by slipping the long ends under the rubber bands.

4. Put a folded paper towel under each leaf. Let the leaf dry several days.

5. Remove the rubber bands and twist ties carefully. Then spray, clear or colored—first inside, let it dry, then the outside.

Skookum Scruffy Happy Hooligan Huston
(INITIALS SSHHH)

Kick It Around

Photo 7

Skookum is a miniature white schnauzer. The breeder raises them because it is thought that they bark less than the black, black and white, or silver ones. There are fewer white schnauzers. His white mother weighed just six pounds. Skookum maintains about fifteen pounds.

Miniature schnauzers are very intelligent. Skookum has a vocabulary understanding of over 125 words or phrases. He realizes when a bath is coming and starts shaking. As an active puppy, he required two or three baths a day, now about weekly or less.

Playing, sleeping, and eating are his main activities. Skookum's biggest joy is to get to go for a ride in the car, even if it is just to put it into the garage at night. When he was young, he would go right to sleep when the car started. Now, at age twelve, he mostly sits up and looks at passing scenery. When outside, every blade of grass has to be sniffed, so walking with him on a leash can be slow and fur around his mouth gets dirty. Dogs have an estimated 200 million scent receptors. Humans only have about 5 million of them.

Tearing up any paper or cardboard in sight shows frustration or anger. Skookum understands the word *No* but may not agree with it. Valuable papers, therefore, go into the car trunk.

Skookum Scruffy Happy Hooligan Huston (SSHHH)

Skookum Scruffy Happy Hooligan
Huston's my name.
SShhh, let's play a game.
Toss a ball past me—I'll run really fast.
It keeps going…
I'll get it at last.
I'll toss it and bite…it's mine alone…
It's *mine*, I say,
'Till I get a bone.
I'll chase the squirrels, tenderly take
Hurt baby bird
My mom to well make.
If our car's involved, I will be good.
Take me with you
Is my attitude.
My dinner I want. I bark at noon.
When bedtime comes,
I bark at the moon.
Pay attention, folks; I want my leash.
But all I hear
Is a firm SShhh-ish.

Springboard Jump

Let's Talk

Does anyone here have a miniature schnauzer?

Who has a dog? What is its name? What color is it?

Who takes care of it?

What has to be done to care for your dog?

How do you know your dog is healthy?

What do dogs eat? When do they eat?

How do you stay healthy?

What can we eat for healthy snacks?

Should dogs have a lot of treats or snacks? Why not?

How do you keep your dog well?

What is *immunization*? Why are dogs immunized?

Are you immunized? For what diseases? Why or why not?

Fun to Do

Let's Share

1. Tell the name of your dog, cat, or other pet, and show a picture.
2. Tell something funny your pet did.

or

3. Tell about something funny you have seen or heard about a pet.

or

Take a Trip to An Animal Shelter

1. Visit a Humane Society animal shelter or foster animal shelter. Afterward, write a short story or poem about your trip.

Jimmycomelately Creek

Kick It Around

Photos 8 & 9

Jimmycomelately creek is near Sequim, Washington. It was named that because a boy named Jimmy would sometimes come when he was expected, but mostly he was late, and sometimes he did not come at all. The *Sequim Gazette* weekly newspaper was named the *Jimmycomelately Gazette* from 1975 to 1991.

Sequim's Jimmycomelately creek bed was changed at one time. The Jamestown S'Kallam Indian Tribe has worked to put the stream water flow back into the original creek bed. They hope the creek will naturally have enough fresh water when the salmon need to swim to or from the Pacific Ocean.

This creek, as pictured, has a *weir* in it. The weir will catch salmon returning in the fall after years of living in the Pacific Ocean. A nearby hatchery will harvest the female salmon eggs, spray the *milt* (male *sperm*) over them, and care for these salmon when they hatch. They will grow in fish hatchery holding ponds until three-inch *fingerlings* are released into Jimmycomelately Creek in the springtime. It is thought that the salmon know to return to where they were released by the smell of the water. This fresh-water creek has a walking bridge (pictured) over it for trail hikers. Fresh water flows into the salt water of Sequim Bay. It continues to flow into the

Strait of Juan de Fuca. Two daily *tides* move this water to and from the Pacific Ocean while the salmon swim.

The Strait of Juan de Fuca is salt water where many kinds of fish swim. It separates part of the U.S.A.'s Washington State from Canada. It is about twenty-five miles wide and used by ships from countries all over the world. The strait is used by commercial, pleasure, and military ocean-going vessels. They go to and from the Pacific Ocean, Puget Sound, and other connected bodies of water. Depending upon size, these ships can *dock* or *moor* at *harbors* in the Strait at Port Angeles, Sequim's John Wayne Marina, or Port Townsend. Continuing into Puget Sound, ships may dock at Everett, Seattle, Tacoma, Shelton, or Olympia (Washington's State capitol).

There is a U.S.A. Navy base in Everett, on the east side of Puget Sound. Additionally, there is a U.S.A. Navy shipbuilding and repair site at Bremerton, on the west side of Puget Sound. Submarines use the Strait of Juan de Fuca to pass under the Hood Canal Bridge. They dock at Bangor Submarine Naval Base located on the east side of the Hood Canal. All of this activity creates waterway military traffic.

People and vehicles cross Puget Sound using the U.S.A.'s largest state-owned ferry system. Small ships and boats can continue from salt-water Puget Sound into fresh-water Lake Washington with shores bordering several cities. There are canal locks in this passage to raise or lower the water level for ships entering or leaving Lake Washington. Salmon climb a fish ladder, which takes them around the locks out of danger when they are going to the Pacific Ocean or returning to their home stream to *spawn* and hatch baby fish.

Jimmycomelately Creek

Some creeks run slowly as you see.
Jimmycomelately runs to the sea.
Sometimes it's slow, when snow melts, fast.
Fingerling salmon hatch at last.

They swim to live far out at sea,
But they'll swim home, just wait and see.
They find Jimmycomelately again to come home.
We're told it's in their chromosome.

Springboard Jump

Let's Talk

How does the name of this creek relate to the boy who could not be relied upon?

Do you remember the story about the boy who called wolf when there was no wolf?

How are these situations similar or different?

During what season of the year do salmon hatch (late winter/early spring)?

What is a fingerling salmon?

When the salmon are big enough to be released at the hatchery, where do they go?

What happens when they go out to sea? Do they swim together?

Would they have fingerlings while at sea? Why?

Why do they always come back to where they were a fingerling?

How can they find where they were hatched?

What is a *chromosome*?

Do we have just one chromosome?

What do chromosomes do?

How can we change our chromosomes?

What happens when fish spawn?

Would water from Jimmycomelately Creek be fresh or salty when it goes into the Strait of Juan de Fuca? Why?

What are tides? What causes them? Would they be all over the world?

Would the U.S.A. Great Lakes have tides? Are they fresh water or salty?

What is the purpose of a protected harbor?

Where and how does a boat dock?

What does it mean to moor a boat or ship? Where can they moor? Why do they moor?

How do locks work to change the seawater level?

What city is the capitol of Washington State?

Fun to Do

Map Reading

1. Look on a map for the Pacific Ocean and the Strait of Juan de Fuca. Find Port Angeles, Sequim Bay, Hood Canal, Puget Sound, Bremerton, Seattle, and Tacoma. Find the passage from Puget Sound into Lake Washington.

or

Trip to a Fish Hatchery

1. Arrange to visit a fish hatchery. Get a tide table (fishing store or newspaper) and learn to read it.

or

Make a Placemat

1. Cut, or better yet tear, a piece of white cloth, like an old sheet or pillow case, in a straight rectangle twelve inches by eighteen inches to use as a placemat. A heavier piece of cloth would be better. Pull threads to make a fuzzy fringe around the cloth.

2. Draw and color a stream with salmon on your placemat using crayons. The stream can have rocks.

Crayon drawings can be made permanent by using an ironing board, with plain heavy paper on *both* sides of your cloth and carefully pressing downward with a warm iron. Lift the iron and repeat until the entire placemat has been pressed. Do not lift or move the paper or cloth on which you are working.

If you use permanent markers, layer heavy paper, like a grocery sack, under your cloth as you paint to protect the tabletop.

Backyard Sanctuary

Kick It Around

Photos 10 & 11

A backyard bird *sanctuary* means that it is a safe place for birds in the backyard. There is usually food and fresh water made available at a home. Sometimes, though, one kind of bird will scare off another kind to get the food. There are many varieties and colors of jays, photo 10, which scare away other birds.

One time, a balcony was *officially* designated as a bird sanctuary. It was several stories up at a lady's home in a big city. The lady took care of many wild birds.

Band tail pigeons that feed below the pictured feeder, photo 11, are larger than a common pigeon. They are gray with a white feather necklace around their neck. Also, look for a broad white stripe near the end of their tails when they fly. They scare easily. Doves coo to their babies called *squabs*. Look for robins digging worms. Many kinds of birds scratch in the ground for fallen seeds. Most birds like suet blocks, which may be bought or made with seeds in them. A large pinecone can be made using suet or peanut butter with seeds pressed between the suet layers or even spread between rough bark on trees. A combination of corn, milo, etc. (chicken scratch) are enjoyed by many birds when scattered on a board under shelter. Squirrels especially like the milo grain.

In Sequim, Washington, the average annual temperature day and night is 40° Fahrenheit as shown on the pictured thermometer. When the ground is frozen or frosty, there will be little for birds to eat in nature. It is good to feed them even in the spring and summer if you want to keep birds coming to your sanctuary. They also need clean water daily. In addition to the interest they create and their beauty, a benefit to helping birds is that they help spread seeds for nature.

Some birds will change their *plumage* feathers' colors during the seasons. These colors usually blend in with their surroundings, making them safer from *predators*. Also, the young may have different colored plumage than the adults.

International Migratory Bird Day is the second Saturday of each May. There may be special celebration events in your city in which you can participate. *Migrating* birds usually fly between 700 and 2,000 feet over the North, Central, and South American lowlands. In Texas, hawks have climbed over 4,000 feet. Birds flying very long distances have been seen rising over Mount Everest and the Himalayan Mountains at 30,000 feet. The highest bird sighting was at 37,900 feet in 1975.

The U.S. Department of the Interior publishes the "State of the Birds Report" annually. In 2011, it reported there are 1,000 bird species in the U.S.A. Another source reports that about 675 species are known to show up annually in North America and our offshore waters. Many are in only one area. We need to take care of birds because 251 of these bird species are in *extinction* danger. Lead from hunter's bullets falling to the ground anywhere can create lead poisoning of the ground worms and other bird food. Animals can die from lead poisoning when they eat food with bullets or lead in it, even years later.

Bird watching is fun. Just like having a pet, wild birds need their food and water regularly, or they won't come back to be watched. Outside, move slowly and do not look straight at the birds or they will think you are a predator who will hurt them. Bird books will help you identify those you see. Remember, your pet cat or dog is usually a predator for birds (see Skookum Scruffy Happy Hooligan (SSHHH).

The "Big Year" movie starring Owen Wilson, Jack Black, and Steve Martin is about birding. It is based upon a non-fiction book by the same name. There are year-long birding competitions, which have been active since 1930. This movie competition and the book relate to activities taking place in 1998.

Backyard Sanctuary

See birds in flight
As eagles soar.
Gold finch twitter
Land by my door.

Migrating geese
In echelon.
Robins searching
For worms on lawn.

Black hood juncos
On the feeder.
Starling flock fears
Hawk in cedar.

Pine siskins flit,
Thistle waiting.
Brown hood cowbirds
Concentrating.

Robins bathing,
Their needs offset.
Band tail pigeons
Imagine threat.

Doves coo in pairs
Quietly eat.
Whistle when fly,
Tuck up their feet.

Screaming blue jays
Scare birds from meals.
Let squirrels appear
To make a steal.

Springboard Jump

Let's Talk

Look at a bird book. How can you find a specific bird to know its name?

Describe a bird's plumage. Is it always the same? What causes differences on the same bird?

Which bird is our national bird? What does it mean that the eagle *soars*?

What animals would be afraid of eagles? Why?

Is an eagle a predator? Would it be a predator to you?

What kind of animal would be a predator looking for you?

Is a person considered an animal? How could a person be a predator to a wild animal?

Do you think these geese would be like the geese in a V in "The Vain Ostrich"?

What does *echelon* mean? Do we ever walk in an echelon?

Why would starlings fear a hawk? What is cedar? What kind of tree?

Has anyone been scratched by a thistle?

What part of the thistle would the pine siskins eat?

Brown hood cowbirds are *concentrating*. What does that mean?

Have we learned to concentrate? When do we concentrate?

What does *threat* mean? What would be a threat to you?

What does "imagine a threat" mean? So, was there really a threat?

What would band tail pigeons do when they think there is a threat to them?

Name things that would be a threat to birds.

What would be a threat to you? Why? What would you do?

What problems would a robin or another bird have that a bath would be needed?

Have you seen a bird take a bath in a puddle? How does a bird take a bath?

Where would birds get a drink of water? Should it be fresh? Why?

Why is there concern if there is an oil spill on water?

Does "doves in pairs" mean they are a family?

HARRIETTE "REE" HUSTON

What would make the whistle sound when they fly away?

Are blue jays quiet birds? How do we know in this poem that they are not quiet?

Why would robins be looking for worms on your lawn after a rain?

What does the squirrel want to eat?

Would the bird food probably be intended for the squirrel?

Is the squirrel afraid of the blue jay?

Can you tell the season of the year from the picture? How?

Why is the thermometer not always a good indication of the season?

Is there a designated official sanctuary for any kind of animal near your home?

What animals are protected?

What are wetlands? Could they be a sanctuary? What could they protect?

Fun to Do

Prepare a Bird Feeder

1. Buy an inexpensive bird feeder. Ask your salesperson what food combination would attract the most birds. Raccoons and mice will eat this seed, if they can get to it, so, either buy a bucket with a tight lid or keep the extra seed inside your home.

2. Hang your feeder. Select a place you can reach so that you can remove it when necessary to clean or refill with seed. A recommended plan to avoid squirrel raids is to place a feeder five feet from the ground, seven feet from any tall plant, wire, or building that could hold the weight of a squirrel, and nine feet under any nearby tree branches.

and

Prepare a Bird Bath

1. Find a way for birds to have a drink of water. It should be large and *shallow* enough that birds can bathe in it. Running water for refill would be best, or change their water daily.

or

"Big Year"

1. See the movie, "Big Year",
and/or

2. Read the book, "Big Year".

WILD RACCOONS

Kick It Around

Photo 12

Raccoons are native to the United States but have been spread over Canada, Europe, and Asia. They can be identified by their black mask around their eyes as well as light and dark bands around their bushy tails, photo 12. Their paws have sharp claws that always stay out on their five individual fingers. They can run, jump, and swim, but not very fast. Long, grayish, coarse fur on their bodies sheds water, but short, thick under-fur keeps them warm. Be careful! They bite often, with sharp teeth. Their memory can last three years.

Christopher Columbus first wrote about raccoons. Pocahontas and her father, Chief Powhatan, called them *algonquin*, pronounced ahra-koon-em, meaning they rub, scrub, and scratch with their hands.

Raccoons give birth to two to four young called *kits* in the springtime in a den. The mother sheds her fur in clumps. These clumps are used to line the den to keep the kits warm. The mother makes sounds to the kits with her thirteen vocal cords. Her kits will leave home in the fall.

A natural curiosity leads wild raccoons to eat everything they can find. A duck could be a fine family meal for them. Bird feeders are routinely emptied by both raccoons and squirrels, unless you use the 5-7-9 placement given in Backyard Sanctuary, Fun to Do. Raccoons will steal and eat wild bird and chicken eggs. They usually look for food at night, but they may be seen during the daytime. Their front paws are calloused. This may explain why they are known to wash their food—they can feel and examine their food better underwater. Their front feet have fingers that can move *expertly*. Just about any lock can be opened, unless it has a key and the key is hidden.

Hunters may still use raccoon meat to eat. The *pelts* (fur) can be made into hats with tails as decorations. (Davy Crockett may have worn one.) The pelts have been made into coats and were high style fashion in the 1920s.

Most wild raccoons only live to be one and a half to three years old. Most are killed by heavy traffic or by licensed hunters. Pets from state licensed breeders may live to be up to sixteen years old. It is not legal to keep a wild raccoon as a pet in most states.

Demanding Raccoons

A mask they wear
So you'll know their look
When they cross the road
To get to a brook.

Dexterous paws
And brains quite agile,
But their lives like ours
Are just as fragile.

If you feed them,
They'll be there on time.
Just meet their schedule
Or your door they'll climb.

They have their homes,
Hungry young to raise.
They might even eat
Duck or mayonnaise.

Unscrew can lids;
Tear open a sack.
'Coons enjoy birdseed
With nuts for a snack.

Preserve with care
All parts of the earth.
We live together
Throughout life from birth.

Springboard Jump

Let's Talk

Where were raccoons first seen in the world?

How could raccoons have started living outside the United States?

Why do we say that a raccoon has a mask?

What is a pelt?

Why would a raccoon want to get to water?

What does their front feet fingers move expertly mean?

What does *dexterous* mean? What do you do to be dexterous? Show us.

What does *agile* mean? How is that different from *dexterous* as used in this poem?

Name something that is *fragile*. So, what does fragile mean? Why is all life fragile?

Why do wild raccoons not live very long? *(review Our Deer Friends)*

How do you know your schedule? Do you have one at home? At school?

How would the raccoon know it was time to be fed?

How do you know it is time to eat?

Why would people call a raccoon a 'coon? Why was 'coon used in this poem?

What would happen if a raccoon climbed your screen door—front or back door?

Why would he climb the door?

Should you bring him food—ever? Why not?

When do you eat mayonnaise?

When would a raccoon eat *mayonnaise*—or duck?

What else might he eat?

What animals would think the raccoon is a predator?

Why was the word mayonnaise used in the poem instead of saying salad dressing?

What is a rhyme? Do all the poems we've read rhyme?

Do they have a beat like a drum?

What is an example of the beat, which is a rhythm?

Does singing have a rhythm? Are some poems in songs? Name some.

How do you take off a lid of a jar? How would the raccoon do it?

If it was a glass jar, what might happen to the jar? Could the raccoon get hurt?

What would the raccoon use to get into a paper or plastic sack?

What is the difference between the claws of a raccoon and a cat?

How would he know to try to get into the sack? Did he read the sack? Why would he want to get in?

Why do we need to be careful taking care of trash and garbage?

How do you protect your trash?

Has any animal ever gotten into it? What happened?

What is meant by preserve with care?

What things do you preserve at home…at school…with friends?

Is the earth the same thing as the world? How do they differ?

What are the gifts of nature in this poem?

Who is living together in this poem?

How would these relationships be peaceful?

How would there be disruption or danger?

Fun to Do

Draw a Raccoon

1. Find another picture of a raccoon. Try looking on the Internet or in a dictionary.
2. Draw a raccoon getting into something at your home. Write or tell about your picture.

Happy Chickens

Kick It Around

Photo 13

Chickens running around have become an uncommon sight. This distinctive wire protecting these chickens is called chicken wire. At night, they safely sleep sitting on stadium-like slats above the ground that go across the inside of their chicken coop (pictured). They tuck their heads under their wing to sleep.

There are many colors of chickens according to the breed, just like there are breeds of dogs. There are several breeds shown in photo 13. Bantam chickens are small, have many varied colors, and lay small delicious eggs. When chickens can run around freely, they are called range chickens.

They may be fed dried corn, either whole kernel, or ground. Eggshells can be fed back to the chickens to help their calcium intake and harden the eggshells when hens lay eggs. They also eat grain and bugs—whatever they can find that other birds haven't eaten.

As a whole, chickens are not usual pets, but an individual one could be considered as such. They cannot be trained as household pets can be. They have a very limited intelligence.

Happy Chickens

A country farm has chickens galore.
Some may run free to nest and explore.
They know when darkness closes the door
To roost in their coop off of the floor.

When daylight breaks, rooster says, me too,
Loud on a fence Cock-A-Doodle-Do!
Everyone wakens to start their day.
Gather eggs nesting hens lay in hay.

Springboard Jump

Let's Talk

Have you seen live chickens?

What colors have they been?

Has anyone had a pet chicken?

What is a mother chicken that lays eggs called? *(hen)*

What could happen to the eggs if a hen runs free? *(look in Wild Raccoons)*

What is a daddy chicken called? *(cock or rooster)*

How can you tell a cock from a hen?

What are baby chickens called? *(chicks)*

What are young hens not a year old called? *(pullets)*

Does darkness really close the door? What does this mean?

What is a chicken coop? Why is it needed?

How is a chicken roost made?

How do chickens roost?

What must the farmer do every night to keep the chickens safe?

Where does the farmer want his hens to lay eggs? *(protected nests)*

Would you be afraid to gather eggs? Why? What might happen?

Are there animals that like to steal and eat eggs? *(weasels, snakes, hawks, raccoons, squirrels)*

Are there animals that will steal and eat chickens, if they can? *(foxes, coyotes, raccoons, hawks, eagles)*

Fun to Do

Hen on a Nest

1. Take about twelve to fourteen inches of lightweight aluminum foil. Roll it loosely and gently crumple (squish) it together lengthwise.
2. Make a beak by carefully pulling out one end just a little bit. Pull out a little more foil and make a small round head behind the beak.

3. Make a short tail pulling out the other end, and make it spread out just a little bit. Crumple the foil between to make an oval body. (When nesting, a hen's neck and feet don't show.)

and

4. Take another square piece of foil and crumple it to make a round nest.

5. Place your hen in the nest.

As the Crow Flies

Kick It Around

Photo 14

Photo 14 was taken early in the morning. There was a huge flock of crows gathered in downtown Bellingham, Washington, in a very large business parking lot. These two crows were sitting in a tree quietly watching all the chattering the others were making on the ground. Crows in the millions have been known to gather with regularity in certain locations. You may hear them saying *caw, caw* to each other.

Crows are much larger than blackbirds. They live everywhere in the lower forty-eight states, in Southern Canada, and south central Alaska. Their feathers are usually a shiny black. They, like many other birds, feed on grain. Crows are also scavengers for meat. They help keep our roadways clean.

When nesting, crows are social like a family to raise their young. The year-olds may help carry nesting twigs, feed the *hatchlings* and caw to alert about danger. About twenty different kinds of birds, including jays, act as a family unit like we do.

Are they intelligent? Many people believe they are. When they were hunted with guns, many moved to safe cities. They learned where to find food in the cities. If they can't crack a nut, they will fly over a road and drop it. If it doesn't break, it is placed for cars to run over it so the nutmeat can be picked up and eaten. Other birds, like the jay, do this, too. Like us, they learn through playing. University of Washington researchers have found that crows learn to know who you are and whether you are nice to them or mean. They'll even teach their young to like you or not.

A small constellation (pattern) of stars in the southern night sky by Virgo is named Corvus (meaning raven or crow). There is a saying, as the crow flies, that refers to going in a straight line to another place. Tall sailing-ship masts usually have a crow's nest. This is a metal basket at the top of the main mast for a sailor to climb up and look long distances. Masts hold the sails of a ship to catch the wind and make the ship move in the water.

As the Crow Flies

Crows meet each day near break of dawn
In trees and on the ground.
My nest needs repair, one will say,
Let's go to the woods and foray.

"Caw, caw," he says and flies away
To find food for today.
I'll carry millet, corn, or bread
So my nesting chicks can be fed.

Black crow struts as he walks the street,
His head bobs front to back,
He appears to be all alone,
But he can fly back to his home.

Springboard Jump

Let's Talk

(Refer to a bird book again.)

What color are crows? How are they different from blackbirds?

What is a convention?

Are the crows having a convention in this poem? Where?

Have you heard the expression, "As the crow flies"?

What does it mean?

What would the crow do to foray? *(search for twigs to take to the nest)*

What is millet? *(small grain and grass seeds—it can be bought at pet stores)*

What other animals eat grain? *(look in Wild Raccoons, Backyard Sanctuary, and Happy Chickens)*

What are the baby crows called?

What other birds have chicks?

What do hatchlings come from? Would all birds have hatchlings?

How does the word *strut* seem like the word *vain* in meaning? *(we called the ostrich vain)*

What do crows do to keep roadways clean?

What other wild animals might help do this job too?

Fun to Do

Pretend You Are a Crow

1. Walk showing us how the crow walks. Now make the *caw caw* sound of a crow. How must it sound at a crow convention?

and

Am I Crowing?

1. People may say that someone crows or brags about an accomplishment. Talk about situations where you could crow about something, and it would be okay.
2. Also, discuss where it would not be okay to crow about the same thing. (see last chapter, "Children, Nature's Gift" chapter, Springboard Jump about accomplishment.)

or

Star Gazing

1. Find a map of star formations. Find Corvus and other star constellations on the map.
2. Find other star formations in the night sky.

Sentinel Trees

Kick It Around

Photo 15

The scene in photo 15 was observed on a roadway as the sun created majestic shadows. The tree shadows are from the tree *sentinels* (guards) of the road. The shadows look so much like the bar codes now used on merchandise in stores. In a store, the bar code holds the information concerning the price of the object in that specific store. Companies make various kinds of computers that read bar codes.

It would seem these shadow bar codes hold the information or secrets of the trees. It tells you there are few leaves on these bare trunks and that there are many trees growing close together. To get such a view would likely be in the country rather than a city where buildings would block such shadows.

When walking on or close to a roadway, *always walk toward traffic* near the road edge white line. The white line on the right of each lane shows the lane edge. A solid yellow line, in the center of the road or in the left side of a driver's lane, shows it is not safe to pass another car in front. In this picture, no car can pass another car going either direction.

Different methods of bar coding are also being utilized. One is coding within a small square that is called a Quick Response Code. These codes connect with smartphones or tablets having apps (many free) to read the code, the phone's internet browser, and the selected website. These Quick Response Codes are square symbols with tiny squares inside of them. QRC originally identified and followed goods during manufacturing. Now they are appearing in advertising to give you more information about the product in which you have interest. They are on envelopes and even on buildings to give you information and *virtual* tours.

Another bar-type code is a thin line of bars that go above and below a center point. There may be more than one type of code on, for instance, a business letter or envelope.

Sentinel Trees

Trees, trees, green trees.
With joy behold spring greens emerge,
Slowly maturing into dark green,
Reflecting early morning dew.

Trees, trees, changing leaves.
Jack Frost painting red and yellow.
Colors falling into swirls.

Trees, trees, ever changing
Evergreens outlined with snow.

Trees, trees, watching
Animals sheltered all year round.

Trees, trees, without leaves.
Shadowy bar codes bare trunks form.
Sentinels of life.

Trees, trees, live so long.
Reddish buds proclaim new life.
Burgeoning branches bloom and spread
Their seeds for trees to grow anew.

Trees, trees, my passion
Watching spring's new greens emerge.

Springboard Jump

Let's Talk

Where should you walk if there is no sidewalk?

When walking on a roadway, why walk toward traffic?

What do you think *sentinel* means? *(to watch over, to guard or protect)*

Why and how would a tree be a sentinel?

Have you seen leaves in the spring as they grow out of branches?

What color are they?

What makes them look green? What makes them darken?

Who is Jack Frost? Is he real? What does it mean, "Colors fall in swirls"?

There are two types of trees. What are they?

How are evergreen trees different from deciduous trees?

How do trees shelter or protect animals?

What animals do they protect?

How do stores use bar codes?

When would bare trees be like bar codes?

Have you ever noticed bar code shadows? Where have you seen a tree bar code?

What are the seasons? How do the seasons affect squirrels and some bats?

Who enjoys watching seasonal changes?

How do you dress differently each season?

Does this poem talk about all the seasons?

What do trees that lose their leaves do in the winter?

What does a burgeoning branch mean to you? *(new growth)*

What would new growth look like? What could come out instead of a leaf?

What does *passion* mean? *("An object of love, deep interest, or zeal." Webster's Collegiate Dictionary)*

Fun to Do

Find Bar Codes

1. Look for bar codes from used products at home. Also, look for a small square of a Quick Response Code and line code. Compare yours with someone else's codes.
2. Notice how they each look different. If you have a smartphone that will respond to the QRC, show how it is operated.

or

Make a Shadow Bar Code

1. Use a square of plastic, firm, florist foam for a base, placed on a much larger white sheet of paper or cloth.
2. Gather small straight sticks that have no leaves or use long toothpicks of different lengths.
3. Place some sticks close together and others farther apart upright in the florist foam.
4. Move the foam with sticks to a darkened area.
5. Shine a bright light at table level toward the sticks. Try different light positions.

    Do you see shadows and how they change?

    Do you see the shadows forming bar codes similar to one you brought from stores?

The Reluctant Mouse

Kick It Around

Photo 16

Mice like to eat cheese. Photo 16 is of a play mouse on a lavender stuffed piece of yellow-cloth cheese. Seeing it will help you in our Fun to Do section after reading this playful poem.

Parents can make up stories about Flipperty mouse and entertain children with a bedtime story after reading the poem to them. The author's children loved hearing the adventures of Flipperty. Babysitters or grandparents will be endeared when they make up Flipperty stories for children.

Toutle was born near the Toutle River in Washington State on the spring day Mt. St. Helens volcano erupted in 1980. The eruption filled the Toutle River with hot ash. It made the river water hot. Toutle was a multicolored female cat that lived to be nineteen years old. She was very good at communicating what she wanted but was not highly intelligent. Which side of the door would open was always a mystery to her.

The Reluctant Mouse

Toutle, my cat, sat by the door all day,
Enjoyed, looked forward to fanciful play.
A reluctant mouse our Flipperty was.
Toutle's fun—chase, catch, and toss him just 'cause.

Flipped in the air, then batted like a ball.
Before that, he wasn't reluctant at all.
Enticing cheese and peanut butter, no.
Let me out of that door without a show!

Springboard Jump

Let's Talk

Who has a cat? How do kittens like to play? What toys do they enjoy?

How do cat and mouse claws differ from raccoon claws? *(review Wild Raccoons)*

What do you think *fanciful* means? Would a toy mouse be fanciful?

Can you figure out what reluctant means?

Why would the mouse be reluctant to show himself?

How did the mouse get the name Flipperty?

Do mice like cheese and peanut butter?

HARRIETTE "REE" HUSTON

Why wouldn't Flipperty eat the food offered?

What was the only thing Flipperty wanted?

What does *endeared* mean? Why would a babysitter want to be endeared?

How will the picture help you to do our activity?

Fun to Do

Map and Articles

1. Look on a map of Washington State for Mt. St. Helens and the Toutle River.
2. Find any articles about this volcanic eruption in 1980.

or

Make a Sachet Mouse

1. Take two pieces of yellow cloth rectangles the same size—ragged edges are okay.
2. Sew them together with a needle and knotted-end thread around the edge about half an inch from the sides, leaving one end open. On the back side, closely sew over and over the last stitch so the thread will not come loose.
3. Partly fill the sack you have made with lavender buds, dried roses, sweet hay, or small grain (no cheese).
4. Sew the rest of the bag closed.

5. Sew big circles in different places in the piece of cheese to hold the filling in place. It will resemble Swiss cheese.

and

6. Make a mouse with a head, long tail, and body like we made a chicken using lightweight aluminum foil. *(see Happy Chickens)*

7. Sew the mouse on the cheese putting several threads over (not through) the neck, body, and tail. Some glue might work in place of sewing.

8. If you used dried lavender or roses for stuffing, place in a drawer to make things smell nice.

Enjoying Creation

Kick It Around

Photo 17

Modern day lavender and other plants have names just as we do. They are even patented. Sequim, Washington's, Lavender Growers Association owns a registered trademark as the "Lavender Capital of North America."

Sunshine is needed for lavender and most other plants to grow and to prevent *fungal* disease. Plants can get sick just as people do. Mushrooms are fungus plants that grow in the dark. *Do not eat* wild mushrooms you see, as most are poisonous.

It is best to water plants during the daytime. They may get mildew, a fungus, from night watering, especially if the air is cool. Fungus can kill plants. Excess water on plants will evaporate more rapidly during warm, sunny summer days than it would during the nighttime. Plants can absorb water through their leaves as well as through their roots. Desert cacti are well known for absorbing moisture from nighttime dew through their leaves. Lavender plants require minimal water.

Scientists are finding many plants show responsive actions. Some know insects that are bad or good for them. Some grow extra long roots to reach water. Electrical impulses have been shown if plants are threatened. Lettuce and bananas have shown results on a lie detector polygraph. Poplar and maple trees have been threatened and other nearby trees have released chemicals to stop the digestion process of predators that might eat their leaves or their bark.

Notice in the following poem that the shape of the printing is like a tree.

Enjoying Creation

Creation
made for daily enjoyment:
Trees
ever changing—spring, summer, fall, and winter,
Shrubs
glistening with rain drops, drinking in sparkling sunlight,
Bees
unseen in winter suddenly busy as spring brings their harvest,
Flowers
that appear one at a time enticing notice of their presence,
Butterflies
like flowers floating heavenward spending their short lives
encased in glory,
Winds
that sing their song year round,
Creation
has its mission, as do each of us.

HARRIETTE "REE" HUSTON

Springboard Jump

Let's Talk

How do plants use the moisture on their leaves?

What is fungus?

What helps fungus grow? Is that good?

What do we eat that is a fungus?

Can we eat all mushrooms? Why not?

Could a dewdrop be water for a bird?

What does *evaporate* mean?

What does *patented* mean? Why are plants patented?

How do you know something is patented? Where are patents issued?

What is a *trademark*?

How would you describe creation?

Can you make creation?

What can you do with it?

What does *harvest* mean? When do farmers harvest crops of wheat and corn?

What do bees harvest?

What is *enticing*? Do you do anything that is enticing? When do you do it?

What things do flowers do to get bees to notice them?

How is a butterfly like a flower? What does a butterfly do for flowers?

What does *encased* mean? How is a butterfly encased in glory? Is it also encased in color?

How does a wind make a song? *(reread "Red Winged Blackbirds' Family and Friends")*

How does the wind help the flowers and other plants?

What is creation's mission?

What is your mission in life; could it change?

Fun to Do

Evaporation Experiment

1. Place a small amount of water on a plate and leave it until it is all gone.
2. Observe it become smaller as it evaporates over time. Why is this important?

or

Make Your Own Butterfly

1. Find a picture of a butterfly. It is an insect having no backbone. It has a body of three parts: head, *thorax* (chest), and *abdomen*. Like other insects, butterflies have three pairs of legs that are attached to its thorax, as do the wings.

2. Using plain heavy paper or a heavy paper grocery sack, draw three slender ovals. Add two thin feelers in front about an inch long at the top of the head.

3. Add butterfly wings using a large triangle shape with a point connecting onto each side of the thorax near the head.

4. Add smaller triangle wings farther back on each side of the body, also, attached to the chest.

5. Add the six legs.

6. Put in the veins of each wing similar to drawing the veins in the leaf done earlier.

7. Be creative with your coloring. Some butterflies have dots and wide borders.

8. Carefully cut out your butterfly.

9. Turn it over, and color the underside laying it on a fresh sheet of paper. It should look like the topside.

10. Fold the wings upward to make it appear to fly.

11. Apply double-side sticky tape underneath the body.

12. Your beautiful butterfly can now appear to fly and stay on a mirror, wall, lampshade, window, or wherever you want to put it—even on your hair. Have fun!

HUMMING BIRD AND CROW

Kick It Around

Photo 18

As in the poem following, a hummingbird did peek in the author's window while being watched. A feeder with special food was then hung from the house eve to encourage repeat visits. Bright colors and sweet-smelling flowers attract these tiny birds. It is best to buy prepared hummingbird food because sugar water will have no needed vitamins and minerals. They need a balanced diet, just like we do. If you can only provide sugar-water, boil and cool four parts water to one part white cane sugar. Do not use honey.

These are the smallest of birds. Sometimes they will briefly sit and rest on a wire fence, stop to sip water or food, or take a very quick dip in the birdbath. Their wings twist as they fly rather than flap like other birds. These wings can act like an airplane rudder. This twist is shown in photo 18. They can fly like no other birds—hover, sideways, forward, backward, and upside down. They have weak legs and feet but can cling to twigs. The sound their wings make is a fast whir sound when they buzz around your head.

Hummingbirds are mainly seen in the spring and summer beginning in April or May, but leave your feeders available until late fall. There are eighteen species in the U.S.A. Some migrate over 2,000 miles between central Mexico to British Columbia,

Canada. This migrating bird's heart can beat up to 1,260 time a minute while their tiny wings move 15 to 80 times a second. It is hard to see their wings when they are flying. One kind stays on the Olympic Peninsula year-round. Their liquid food may freeze in the winter, so feeders need extra attention. All birds need water in the winter, too.

Two bean-sized eggs are laid and incubated in tiny cup-shaped nests the female humming-bird builds out of plant fibers and spider webs. Some species will return to that particular nest or even build a new one over the old one. If they like you, they will be back next year.

Humming Bird and Crow

Curious humming bird,
Peeking in my window.
We join in love
For sweet flowers.

His quiet presence
In my life
Adds cherished memories.
Hear the raucous crow?

Springboard Jump

Let's Talk

Do you see the humming bird's twist in its wing?

What is similar on an airplane wing? How does an airplane use its flaps on the wing? On the tail?

What does the word *curious* mean? Are you ever curious? What do you do?

What game do we play with babies that involves peeking?

Do hummingbirds like flowers? Why?

Why do you like flowers? Have you ever sipped nectar from a honeysuckle vine?

What does *cherished* mean?

What is a memory?

What would be a cherished memory?

Name some cherished memories you have.

Raucous means what in this poem? Who is being raucous? Let's spell raucous.

Would a football game likely be raucous?

Where else would you hear something raucous?

What is the tiniest bird in the world?

Can you name the tallest living flying bird? *(look in The Vain Ostrich)*

Can you name the largest living bird that doesn't fly?

Fun to Do

Word Meanings

1. Write down other words with similar meanings to raucous.
and
2. Discuss or write in a few sentences showing how these words differ in meaning.

Let's Go Batty

Kick It Around

Photo 19

Bracken Cave close to San Antonio, Texas, has the largest grouping of mammals, which are Mexican free-tailed bats. About twenty million bats of one species are there. Bats are important mammals because they eat tons of insects that would otherwise overrun the earth. There are about 1,100 species of bats over the earth, which accounts for about 20 percent of all mammals. Their size can start from 1.14 inches in length (smaller than your thumb) and they can have up to a 5-foot wingspan.

Do not handle any bat—ever! Like mice, they can carry disease. On the East Coast of the U.S.A. and Canada, scientists are worried about a new bat disease. It is a fungus called white nose syndrome or Geomyesdectructants. People do not get this disease.

Bats are the only true flying mammals. They give birth to their young, whereas birds lay eggs and hatch their young. They have thin wings for forearms on which the fungus may grow. They may have up to two finger-like claws on each hand. Back feet are used to cling to a branch or inside a hanging bat house from the top or sides positioned upside down to sleep. They must store fat to hibernate during the winter. Some bats will migrate and then hibernate.

This new fungus awakens them from hibernation. They will be unable to find food so they die or freeze. The fungus, like bats, lives best in low temperatures and high *humidity*. Hibernation lowers bats' breathing, body temperature, and heart rate, so that they can live. About 24 of 45 species in the U.S.A. and Canada hibernate.

Many bats have good sight, but others use mostly *echolocation* (sound bouncing back from objects) with their ears like dolphins and whales. They also communicate by sound. All bats seldom fly in the rain because the sounds made by the rain prevents them from hearing. Their sense of smell is good.

About 70 percent of the bats eat insects; about 25 percent feast on fruits, nectar, and pollen; there are a few in South America that will eat small birds, mammals, or fish. A good thing they do is pollinate flowers and spread seeds to grow, as well as eat insects.

Mother bats usually have only one baby pup each year, but father bats do not stay around to help raise the young. Pups can't fly until they are two to four months old. They are fully grown in about two years. Bats can live over twenty years, generally in the same place. They do not change where they live easily.

Let's Go Batty

Bats, you know, hang upside down
To sleep away the day,
Then fly at night and insects eat
For winter fat to stay.

Winter hibernation sleep
Will last 'til springtime comes.
When insects hatch and search to eat,
The bats can overcome.

The farmer needs you—wake up!
He's planted special seed.
Flying insects find juicy plants.
They'll eat the crops with greed.

Bats awake to rescue plants
The insects would devour.
So have a bat house for their sleep,
And your yard they'll scour.

Springboard Jump

Let's Talk

What designated day on the calendar makes us think of bats? How big can some bats become?

Where do bats live?

Why do we want bats around our yards? What good would the bats do?

Is that a real bat shown in the picture? Why do you think it is not real?

What are mammals? Why are bats called mammals?

Name some other mammals.

Why would bats live in a cave? Would you see bats during the day? Why not?

Should you pick up a bat? Why not?

What does hibernate mean? How long does it last?

Do you hibernate?

Why does this new disease kill a bat?

What are baby bats called?

Who takes care of them?

How long can a bat live?

What other animals store fat for winter so that they can hibernate?

HARRIETTE "REE" HUSTON

Do insects hibernate? What makes them come out, even in winter?

Would the warmth waken the bats to eat them?

The word *'til* has an apostrophe. Why?

What is a contraction? What word has been shortened?

Why were contractions used in this poem?

How do bats rescue juicy plants?

What does *devour* mean? Can you get the meaning from the way devour is used?

Is this a way to learn new words—by noticing how they are used?

From the usage, what do you think *scour* means? What gives you clues?

Fun to Do

Compare a Bat and a Butterfly

1. Find a picture of a bat.
2. Looking at a picture of a bat, how does the shape of a bat differ from a butterfly?

and

Create a Bat Family

1. Draw your own outline of a bat on heavy black paper, or color it black on heavy paper, like a paper grocery sack. It

will have a body, head, front legs webbed to the end of the body, and back legs. Make some bigger than others. You now have a bat family. Stick them on plants for fun like you did with your previous butterfly. *(see Enjoying Creation)*

or

Hang a Bat House

1. To encourage bats, make or buy a bat house, photo 19. It needs to be open at the bottom and be made of roughed-up or cedar wood so they can sleep hanging upside down inside clinging with their claws to the rough house boards. Ten to twelve bats can occupy the same bat house.
2. Hang the bat house. It needs to be where the south sun warms it, and it should have no shade.

A STITCH IN TIME

Kick It Around

Photo 20

Photo 20 is an example of a beautiful California quail eggshell identified by the Dungeness River Audubon Center, Sequim, Washington. It is creamy white with golden splotches of many sizes. These shy quail scuttle around together quickly in a *covey* (group) to hide in bushes. They do noisy scratching and make soft sounds. California quail have a distinctive forward-facing feather plume.

Killdeer are a widespread shore bird in the Pacific Northwest. They make their nests on the ground, on gravel, lawns, pastures, and even gravel roofs of houses. Killdeer eggs look similar to this quail egg but are larger. Both blend with their surroundings.

Many birds will pretend to be hurt to get the attention of anything that might harm their nest and eggs. Once the adult bird has the attention of a predator, it will lead the predator away from the nest. When the predator is safely led away from the nest, the adult bird will fly away from the predator.

Notice in the following poem that the first line presents a difficult situation. The second line counters with the positive overcoming the negative.

A Stitch in Time

A fallen tree
Lets green grass see.

A broken bird egg, nest forlorn,
New life looks for a little corn.

Meals are work to make and bake,
Friends will bond as all partake.

Lightning forms in clouds' décor,
Delay your trip to the store.

Car breaks down; delay ensues,
Hitch a ride a day or two.

Dirty laundry hard to hold—
Washed, feels and smells fresh to fold.

Love our pets; they need our care.
In return get joy—that's fair.

Music hits a sour note,
Next time as composer wrote.

Feel depressed, dark, and alone?
Call God on his telephone.

HARRIETTE "REE" HUSTON

Love each other, harsh words ne'er,
For them there is no repair.

Springboard Jump

Let's Talk

What does it mean to be negative? To be positive?

What do trees do that stops grass from growing?

What does the word *scuttle* mean?

What does nest forlorn mean? *(review Backyard Sanctuary and Wild Raccoons.)*

The tiny bird hatched and is gone, so why would it look for corn?

What does *partake* mean? How is that similar to the bird looking for corn?

Why do people like to eat together? What can we do to help prepare meals?

Why not go outside during a storm and lightening? What could happen?

If you are swimming and a storm comes, what should you do?

Hitch a ride means what?

Who would you hitch a ride with?

Why should all ages of people leave a note at home telling who you are with, the time of day, where you are going, and when to expect you home?

Should you, a child, get permission from your parents before hitching a ride? Why should you?

What is laundry? How can we help with laundry?

How do we take care of our pets? Why do we even want or have pets?

What is a sour note? How is it like sour candy?

Would the composer have written a sour note? How did it get there?

How do you feel if you are depressed? When should you expect to feel depressed?

Is a prayer God's telephone? What could you say?

Is there really any person there to speak back to you?

Should you talk to your parents if you feel depressed?

Ne'er has an apostrophe, making it a contraction. Is this word used very often?

Why was ne'er used here? *(one syllable for what was a two-syllable word)*

What could happen if you speak harsh words? Give examples of harsh words.

Why would there be no repair for harsh words?

Have you heard the saying, "If you can't say something nice, don't say anything at all"? Why is that good advice?

Fun to Do

Compliments

1. Each person write something nice about the person next to you. Write your friend's name and the date at the top of your paper. Include why you think this is nice and why you like it. Sign your name.

and

2. Exchange papers with an unnamed person. One at a time, each person read aloud these nice written comments received with the written name. Then, give the paper you hold to your friend.

or

Help Our Birds or Protect Plants

1. Save dried crushed chicken eggshells so that you can make them available to nesting birds. The calcium in them can help strengthen the new bird eggshells when they are laid. A restaurant cook might be willing to save eggshells for you, if you ask. Be sure to pick them up on time when the cook wants you to do so.

2. Put crushed eggshells around tender outdoor plants that slugs like to eat. Yard slugs will not move over crushed eggshells. This is another way to use all of your crushed eggshells.

In the Still of the Night

Kick It Around

Photo 21

Frogs

Have you seen a real live frog? Where is the frog in the photo 21?

Live frogs (*amphibians*) live all over the earth. There are over six thousand *species* (kinds). Most live in fresh water, on the ground, in trees, or in burrows. Long legs make it possible for them to jump, and some have webs between their toes to help with swimming. They have four toes on the front feet and five toes on their back feet. Toads are frogs with short legs for hopping or tree climbing and, usually, are brown with rough tough skin. Toads can live further from water than most frogs, due to their thicker skin helping them keep moisture.

Color among frogs may vary. The skin color may change on some frogs to warn of poisonous skin. Some get their poisons by eating ants and mites. Color may also help to change the amount of heat being absorbed. A color change may be used to make them blend into their surroundings and protect them.

Frogs use their skin in many other ways. They absorb and release water and sometimes even breathe through their skin. When frogs are underwater, they get oxygen through their skin. On land, they use their type of lung, which is part of their skin. Their kidney function is also in their skin. All frogs shed their skin regularly and most eat it.

Different species make different sounds. If a lot of males call together, it is called a chorus. This is usually done with their mouth closed. A call for help is made with their mouth open. Some male frogs in Texas, Mexico, and Costa Rica make sheep-like *bleats* to call mates.

Female frogs lay eggs, called *spawn*, in fresh water—even in a puddle. When they hatch, they are called *tadpoles* or *polliwogs*. They have tails, gills, and fins. When they change into adults, losing their tails, gills, and fins, it is called metamorphosis. Then, as juveniles they are called *froglets*, and they develop four legs.

What do they eat? Polliwogs eat algae plants, but adult frogs eat insects and bugs. The insect is held in the adult's mouth with teethlike structures until swallowed whole. But first, and this is hard to believe, the frog *squashes down his eyeballs* to allow the food to go down his throat. Frogs in cold climates may live 12 years, but lowland frogs will likely live only five years.

There are many endangered species because of a fungal infection called chytridiomycosis (chytrid for short). In 2009, this infection was found on all continents, in forty-three countries, and reported in thirty-six states in the U.S.A. It is found on frogs from the hot tropics to the top of 11,000-foot high Sierra Nevada Mountains in California. When they become adults, they are more likely to get chytrid. There are a few kinds that do not get this disease. Scientists are very worried about the survival of many kinds of frogs.

Some frog and toad skin poisonous secretions and nutrient proteins are being examined for possible pain medicines and new antibiotics. New ways may become possible for treating cancer, diabetes, stroke, and organ transplants. It is possible more than one billion people worldwide may have help with 70 major health problems.

Owls

Owls are called birds of prey. They eat insects and small rodents, like mice. They also tend to keep away other birds from harming crops. Farmers may put fake owls around their fields, much like using scarecrows.

Owls are known for their nighttime *(nocturnal)* activity and call of whooo, whooo to each other. Barred owl calls sound like, Who cooks for you? Who cooks for you all? You might even hear an eastern screech owl. Hunting will occur day and night if they are hungry for prey. The short-eared owl always hunts this way.

Some adult owls (the northern saw-whet) are as small as eight inches long; others (the long-eared) have tufts of plumage on the top of their heads that make them fifteen inches long. Barn owls are identified by their pale heart-shaped faces. Nests of burrowing owls are only found in Florida and the western half of the U.S.A. Great gray owls may use old nests of other birds to lay, usually, two to four eggs in early springtime. All owl chicks, or owlets, hatch with white feather down and their eyes closed like newborn kittens.

Owls hear well. This is because their facial feathers direct sound to their ears on the sides of their heads.

People may treat their yards with iron phosphate (the working ingredient in some eco-friendly lawn treatment products. Iron phosphate can feed plants, kill slugs, but not harm birds, toads, or pets. Other biological eco-friendly products are also on the market. Some insects that might be killed are beneficial in some ways, but may cause some damage in other ways. Owls may eat some of these treated animals. Read and reread all product labels before using them.

Some *pesticides* can kill birds, fish, honeybees, and amphibians. Some (glyphosate) do not hurt fish but are deadly to frogs. There are no requirements for pesticides to be tested on amphibians which includes frogs.

In the Still of the Night

See the night?
Hear the silence?
Is it not total?

A dog barks
In the distance.
Brilliant moonlight.

A brief patter of rain droplets.
Croaking frogs.
An owl hoots.

Sudden awareness—
A fast moving stream?
Distant traffic.

Water softener
Regenerates.
A bedspring squeaks.

Moonlight breaks through,
A golden pathway upon the water,
Stretch with big yawn.

Sleep is needed.
Back to bed.
Yes, all is well.

Springboard Jump

Let's Talk

What was the weather like in the first part of the poem?

Did the weather change? What happened?

What animals said they liked the rain? How did they say they liked the rain?

Would you pick up a frog or toad? Why not?

What are frog eggs called? Have you seen a tadpole or polliwog? Tell about it.

What would the owl be looking for at night? What do they do during the day?

Have you ever been up in the night and experienced the silence? What is it like?

Why is it usually considered silent at night?

Are you surprised when you hear noise?

What noises are heard in the poem? What other noises have you heard at night?

What happens when there is noise at night?

Can you get used to sleeping through noise?

What broke the silence?

What is traffic?

How was the sound of a stream created? Was there really a stream?

What other sounds were heard?

What happens when a water softener regenerates?

Was there anyone else in the house? How do you know?

Did the weather change again? How do you know?

Where did the moon have to be in the sky for there to be a golden pathway?

Would that be the moon's sunset? Was there probably a stream or lake there?

Was everything peaceful again?

What could the person in the poem do instead of going back to bed?

How would you then feel the next day?

How would it affect what you did during the day?

How much sleep do you need?

Does everyone need the same amount of sleep?

Fun to Do

Golden Pathway

1. Draw a night picture of the water with the golden pathway on it. The moon would be near the water or low mountains.

or

Owl Head

1. Find a picture of a barn or barred owl—or one with no tufts that look like ears. Notice that, like the northern spotted owl, the ears do not show. Color or paint the head of an owl on a round, flattened, paper plate or round, flattened, heavy coffee filter.

or

A Map Treasure Hunt

1. On a world map find where there are countries with hot tropics and find the cold Sierra Nevada Mountains in the U.S.A. Also, find Texas, Mexico, and Costa Rica.

Teamwork

Kick It Around

Picture in your mind's eye your friends doing a project together with you. This poem likens the teamwork of a group of people to the action of raindrops. The team could be a family, a work-related group with a common purpose, a school group, or an organization. The group would be seeking to make improvements with a specific project.

Not all actions will result positively; therefore, exploration that becomes trial and error is needed. We can utilize the work of others done previously to save time and effort, therefore, speeding the process. Some actions will cause major improvements that will be seen by others.

Raindrops join together, becoming a body of water, perhaps very small or even very large. Their paths are especially noticeable on a car's front window while driving. Rain runoff has been collected as a source of soft water for washing. Rain runoff from land goes into streams (some are underground), rivers, and eventually into an ocean. If the runoff is from farm animals, it can create risk for disease in nearby water. Safe drinking water is called *potable* water.

People work together setting goals to guide them until the project is completed. Some projects will be short term; others will be long term. A family can have short-term goals, but family life is long term. The family includes those who have lived and gone before you. They are called ancestors or forefathers.

Forefathers Day, December 22, is the anniversary of the Pilgrim fathers (including women and children) who landed at Plymouth, Massachusetts, in 1620.

Thanksgiving, the last Thursday in November, is now celebrated each year, including the Pilgrims with praise to God for goodness and mercy.

Teamwork

Like unto the raindrops,
Preparing to immerse.

Some are moving, feigning
As they journey onward,
Like a school child seeking
Explores with disregard.

Some will drift, others sweep
Their changes on ahead,
When gone we clearly see
A brightness in their stead.

By treading well-worn paths,
Forefathers cleared aside,
Our progress takes a jump
In visions and in pride.

When we join together,
Our mission to complete,
Unknown strength emerges,
The whole performs a feat.

Our souls like raindrops join
In God's great universe.

Springboard Jump

Let's Talk

What does using your mind's eye mean?

How is using your mind's eye like remembering?

What other things could you picture in your mind's eye?

How do people immerse themselves without getting into water?

Is moving always a forward motion?

What does *feigning* mean?

When do you pretend to do something, but it is teasing? You won't really do it.

How is soft water different from hard water?

How does drifting or sweeping relate to leadership?

Who are our forefathers?

Why are they important to us?

What is a vision in relationship to a goal or a statement of mission?

How does strength emerge?

What would be an example of a *feat*?

How else could feat be spelled? What is the difference between feat and feet?

Fun to Do

Disregarding Consequences

1. Tell an example of exploring with disregard to the consequences.

and

2. Draw a picture of a dangerous activity. Draw another picture of a helpful activity. Write a story about your drawings including how cooperation was important in each project. Include the project goals.

and/or

HARRIETTE "REE" HUSTON

Raindrops Map

1. Find and discuss the continental divide in relationship to the raindrops' movement. Refer to a map of the United States tracing the movement of water from the continental divide to an ocean.

Children, Nature's Gift

Kick It Around *Photo 22*

Children are nature's gift desired by many people. Each day, parents spend most of their waking time doing something that will benefit either their own children or the children in their lives. Parents do work from which they have money to buy the essentials or even nonessentials for children. People do not always see the results of their generosity. They may donate money to charities that benefit children. Some include their own children in the process of buying gifts for children in other countries where there is great need. Community organizations, the military, and church groups often furnish gifts of food and toys to children in need. Children want to be remembered. They want to be held in high esteem at all ages and be considered of great value.

Singing by children is a blessing enjoyed by many people, including the performers. Schools have choirs and bands to assist the learning process. Sports and competitions are encouraged to help school children develop physically and emotionally. Adults go to school to learn to teach children. Clothing is made for them either in manufacturing processes or lovingly created at home. Medicines are researched and manufactured to preserve the health of children (as well as adults).

Our society and government entities have primary concerns for the well-being of the children of our country. Sometimes, parents are unable to obtain the bare essentials for even their own children. There are private and governmental entities to which they can turn to for help.

Parents shop for nutritious food and make balanced meals to protect their children. A treat of cookies made at home, perhaps with the help of a child, will say that they are remembered and loved.

The following poem includes the actual delicious drop-cookie recipe used to make the cookies pictured, photo 22. Each ingredient is related to the action of the people involved. Compacting brown sugar, to measure it, is like sharing the love of Jesus. Put all your might into it, pour it all out, and share the results. The joy experienced will be returned in full measure.

Each ingredient must be active and do its part in order to make a wholesome, delicious cookie. Children are very active, which helps them to develop well-rounded personalities. Among things that parents are responsible for are giving love, healthful food, and developmental activities. All of these are necessary for children to accomplish their successful growth into adulthood. This process of growing up brings joy to the heart of a parent.

Cookies 'n Kids

Take two big eggs—two boys or more,
One cup brown sugar—can play outdoors.
Flour one point five cups—sand pile too,
A sprinkle of salt—a smile or two.
Cinnamon one t.—laughs add spice,
Sift them together—they come out nice.
Add cup chopped nuts, floured—pockets, sew.
Oven; grease pan, flour too—watch them grow,
Orange juice (1.5 t.) plus zest—hear playful sounds.
Now beat together—they run around,
Chop half-cup gumdrops, floured—book read.
Top before bake—snack, prayer, then bed,
Drop by teaspoons—turn out the light,
Fifteen min., 325°—sleep tight.
Two dozen cookies—share with friends,
or cut 8-x-8 bars—dreams, pretend.
Now sit and rest—your work is done,
Coffee and cookie—what joy a son!

Springboard Jump

Let's Talk

How could you be like one of the ingredients in this recipe?

How else do you eat eggs?

What other foods have flour?

Are there different kinds of flour? Name some of them.

Why do we drink orange juice?

What other foods should we eat each day?

When would cookies, such as these, be served?

Why would just eating cookies and candy not be good for you?

What age group would the children described be?

Name some games that would be outdoors?

What age group would enjoy a sand pile?

What do children do when they are happy?

How do we know these children are happy?

What are indicators of growth?

Why are they important?

Why are pockets important to a child?

What could need to be sewn?

What would be a good bedtime snack?

Why should the snack be low in sugar?

Could the book being read be similar to this book?

Why do people like to read before going to sleep?

Why is sleep important? How much sleep should different age people have?

How do you feel accomplishment from a day's work? What is a child's work?

What would you say to someone else to convey an accomplishment?

(see the chapter, As the Crow Flies, Fun to Do)

Why must you be careful how to talk with someone about your accomplishment?

What is joy? How is love part of joy?

How do you show love or joy?

What do parents do for their children?

How do parents show love?

How do you show love to people around you?

Fun to Do

Make Cookies

1. Make these cookies (the recipe is in the poem) and enjoy them. Remember, they should be soft, so bake for about twelve to fifteen minutes. They will be dry and hard if baked longer. They do not brown. Store tightly covered when cool. Refrigeration or freezing is best.

and

2. Share them with family or friends. *(Note: if you have stored sugar cookies to be served later, do not store these cookies in the same package—see The Vain Ostrich, Fun to Do, Decorate Sugar Cookies.)*

or

Trip to a Grocery Store

1. Make a trip to the grocery store. Find crackers or snacks made with rice or other grains. Look for different kinds of flour to buy including rice, cornmeal, tapioca, barley, whole wheat, etc.

2. Note: Arizona residents are starting to use flour made from the pods and seeds of *mesquite*. It is a *legume* plant that puts *nitrogen* back into the soil. Mesquite flour is *gluten*-free and useful for some cooking. Gluten (in wheat and some other grains) makes some people sick.

3. Write a story about your trip.

Create a Garden

1. Plant a garden—even in planters. Paper egg cartons with good soil can be used to start seeds in late winter indoors. To *transplant*, cut the carton apart and plant in outdoor soft ground soil, usually in May. Be sure to water new growth daily. *(the egg carton will dissolve)*

BIBLIOGRAPHY

Publications

All the Birds of North America: 1997, by American Bird Conservancy and Jack L. Griggs.

Audubon, magazine: July/August 2011: Pretty Poisons, page 14; Missing the Mark, page 15; Galloping Ahead, A Conversation with the Interior Department Chief, page 18; Plant Smarts, page 20; Sheep in Frog's Clothing, page 37; Paradise Found (Cambodia), pages 50-56. May/June 2011: Bug Off! #8 Slugs, pages 40-44; March/April 2011: Sniff Test and How High Do Migrating Birds Fly?, page 28; Urban Planting, page 50; Rice Makes Might, page 68; Bats Up, page 91; Flour Power, page 92; Biotech, page 102.

Birds & Blooms, magazine: October/November 2011: Bird Tales, page 18; Unwanted Houseguest, page 22; In Pursuit of the Hoot, pages 25-31; Extreme Birding, pages 32-34; August/September 2011: Walk This Way, page 18; Ruby Throated Hummingbird, page 41; April/May 2011: Chemical Free Control, page 15; Helpers at the Nest, page 21; Seed Mix on Steroids, page 31; A Soft Spot for CROWS, pages 46-48; Regional Reports: South Central, page 58, and Northwest, page 59; December/January 2011: Roosting Habits, page 23; October/November 2010: George's Corner Fall Birding Checklist, page 19; Nectar lovers, page 45; the secret lives of OWLS, pages 46-58; did you know? page 66.

Birds of Seattle and Puget Sound: 1996, by Chris C. Fisher.

Jeopardy, Television Show: A baby dove is a squab, May 20, 2011.

National Geographic, magazine: April 2011: Indomitable Snow Frogs, pages 139-145; December 2010: Crash: Bat Crisis. April 2009: The Vanishing Amphibians, pages 138 through 153.

The Nature Conservancy: 4245 N. Fairfax Drive, Suite 100, Arlington, VA 22203, May 2011.

The Orchard Mason Bee: 1993, by Brian L. Griffin, Bellingham, Washington.

Peninsula Daily News, newspaper: August 8, 2011: QRC to www.peninsuladailynews.com.

Sequim This Week, newspaper: March 11-17, 2009: Cartoon "Ask Shagg" by Peter Guren.

The Valley News: July 2011, John L. Scott Real Estate: Karen Pritchard, Volume 11, Issue 2: QR Codes: Sign of the Times.

Washington Atlas & Gazetteer: First Edition 1988, DeLorme Mapping Company.

Webster's Collegiate Dictionary: Fifth Edition 1936, G. & C. Merriam Co., Publishers, Springfield, Mass., U.S.A.

Internet

http://www.Exploratorium.edu/frogs/mainstory/frogstory2.html. June 2011.

http://www.TheFrog.org/biology/skin. June 2011.

http://www.Ivanhoe.com. (Ivanhoe Newsite), Queen's University Belfast, Belfast, Ireland, June 7, 2011.

I Care Books

Nature's Gifts A Family Fun Book Exploring
Pictures, Prose, & Poetry for All Ages
www.tatepublishing.com
(eBook also available)

The Rescue of Buster Bus A True Adventure Mystery
with Sparkling Intrigue for All Ages,
www.xlibrispublishing.com

Grandma's 1893 Cook Book
Upcoming

To Order

Utilize Your Local Book Store or
Contact Ree Huston
Toll Free Phone: 888-270-9554
http://www.ICareBooks.com
E-mail: Ree@ICareBooks.com